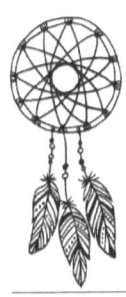

# Dream Journal

I0491000

Date:_____          Time:_____

## Thoughts Before Sleep

_____
_____
_____
_____
_____

## Emotions Before Sleep

_____

## Dream

_____
_____
_____
_____
_____
_____
_____

## Interpretation

_____
_____
_____

## Feeling Upon Awakening

_____
_____
_____
_____

## Comments

_____
_____
_____

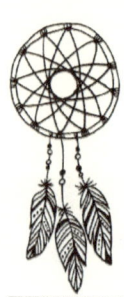

# Dream Journal

Date:_____     Time:_____

## Thoughts Before Sleep

_____
_____
_____
_____
_____

## Emotions Before Sleep

_____

## Dream

_____
_____
_____
_____
_____
_____
_____
_____

## Interpretation

_____
_____
_____

## Feeling Upon Awakening

_____
_____
_____

## Comments

_____
_____
_____

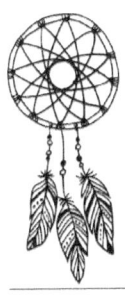

# Dream Journal

Date:_____          Time:_____

## Thoughts Before Sleep

_____
_____
_____
_____
_____

## Emotions Before Sleep

_____

## Dream

_____
_____
_____
_____
_____
_____
_____
_____

## Interpretation

_____
_____

## Feeling Upon Awakening

_____
_____
_____

## Comments

_____
_____
_____

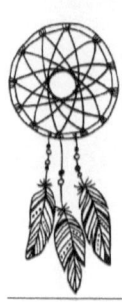

# Dream Journal

Date:_____          Time:_____

## Thoughts Before Sleep

_____
_____
_____
_____
_____

## Emotions Before Sleep

_____

## Dream

_____
_____
_____
_____
_____
_____
_____

## Interpretation

_____
_____
_____

## Feeling Upon Awakening

_____
_____
_____

## Comments

_____
_____
_____

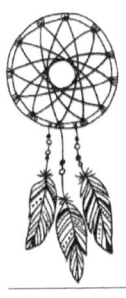

# Dream Journal

Date:_____          Time:_____

## Thoughts Before Sleep

_____
_____
_____
_____
_____

## Emotions Before Sleep

_____

## Dream

_____
_____
_____
_____
_____
_____
_____

## Interpretation

_____
_____

## Feeling Upon Awakening

_____
_____
_____

## Comments

_____
_____
_____

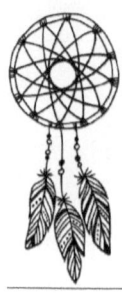

# Dream Journal

Date:_____          Time:_____

### Thoughts Before Sleep

_____
_____
_____
_____
_____

### Emotions Before Sleep

_____

### Dream

_____
_____
_____
_____
_____
_____
_____
_____

### Interpretation

_____
_____
_____

### Feeling Upon Awakening

_____
_____
_____

### Comments

_____
_____
_____

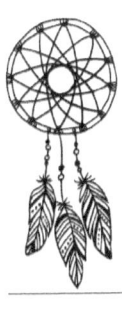

# Dream Journal

Date:_____          Time:_____

## Thoughts Before Sleep

_____
_____
_____
_____

## Emotions Before Sleep

_____

## Dream

_____
_____
_____
_____
_____
_____
_____

## Interpretation

_____
_____

## Feeling Upon Awakening

_____
_____
_____

## Comments

_____
_____
_____

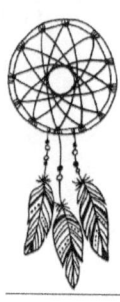

# Dream Journal

Date:_____          Time:_____

## Thoughts Before Sleep

_____
_____
_____
_____
_____

## Emotions Before Sleep

_____

## Dream

_____
_____
_____
_____
_____
_____
_____

## Interpretation

_____
_____
_____

## Feeling Upon Awakening

_____
_____
_____

## Comments

_____
_____
_____

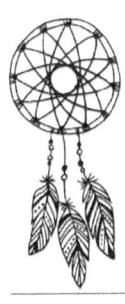

# Dream Journal

Date:_____          Time:_____

## Thoughts Before Sleep

_____
_____
_____
_____

## Emotions Before Sleep

_____

## Dream

_____
_____
_____
_____
_____
_____
_____

## Interpretation

_____
_____
_____

## Feeling Upon Awakening

_____
_____
_____

## Comments

_____
_____
_____

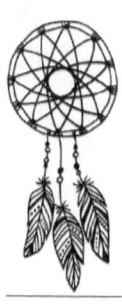

# Dream Journal

Date:_____          Time:_____

## Thoughts Before Sleep

_____
_____
_____
_____
_____

## Emotions Before Sleep

_____

## Dream

_____
_____
_____
_____
_____
_____
_____

## Interpretation

_____
_____
_____

## Feeling Upon Awakening

_____
_____
_____
_____

## Comments

_____
_____
_____

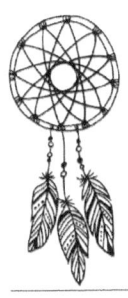

# Dream Journal

Date:_____          Time:_____

## Thoughts Before Sleep

_____
_____
_____
_____
_____

## Emotions Before Sleep

_____

## Dream

_____
_____
_____
_____
_____
_____
_____
_____

## Interpretation

_____
_____
_____

## Feeling Upon Awakening

_____
_____
_____

## Comments

_____
_____
_____

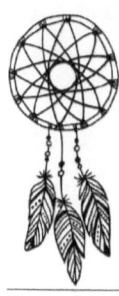

# Dream Journal

Date:_____          Time:_____

## Thoughts Before Sleep

_____
_____
_____
_____
_____

## Emotions Before Sleep

_____

## Dream

_____
_____
_____
_____
_____
_____
_____

## Interpretation

_____
_____

## Feeling Upon Awakening

_____
_____
_____

## Comments

_____
_____

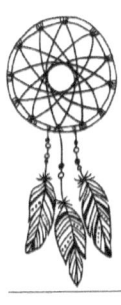

# Dream Journal

Date:_____          Time:_____

## Thoughts Before Sleep

_____
_____
_____
_____
_____

## Emotions Before Sleep

_____

## Dream

_____
_____
_____
_____
_____
_____
_____

## Interpretation

_____
_____

## Feeling Upon Awakening

_____
_____
_____

## Comments

_____
_____
_____

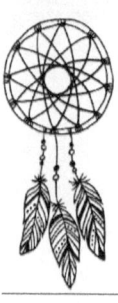

# Dream Journal

Date:_____  Time:_____

## Thoughts Before Sleep

_____
_____
_____
_____
_____

## Emotions Before Sleep

_____

## Dream

_____
_____
_____
_____
_____
_____

## Interpretation

_____
_____

## Feeling Upon Awakening

_____
_____
_____

## Comments

_____
_____
_____

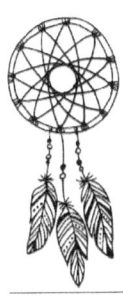

# Dream Journal

Date:_____          Time:_____

## Thoughts Before Sleep

_____
_____
_____
_____
_____

## Emotions Before Sleep

_____

## Dream

_____
_____
_____
_____
_____
_____
_____

## Interpretation

_____
_____

## Feeling Upon Awakening

_____
_____
_____

## Comments

_____
_____
_____

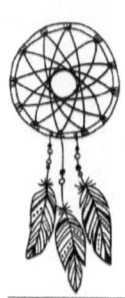

# Dream Journal

Date:_____                    Time:_____

## Thoughts Before Sleep

_____
_____
_____
_____
_____

## Emotions Before Sleep

_____

## Dream

_____
_____
_____
_____
_____
_____
_____

## Interpretation

_____
_____
_____

## Feeling Upon Awakening

_____
_____
_____

## Comments

_____
_____
_____

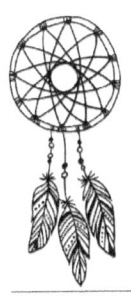

# Dream Journal

Date:_____          Time:_____

## Thoughts Before Sleep

_____
_____
_____
_____
_____

## Emotions Before Sleep

_____

## Dream

_____
_____
_____
_____
_____
_____
_____
_____

## Interpretation

_____
_____
_____

## Feeling Upon Awakening

_____
_____
_____

## Comments

_____
_____
_____

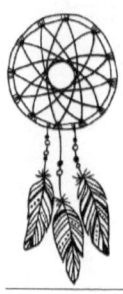

# Dream Journal

Date:_____ Time:_____

### Thoughts Before Sleep

_____
_____
_____
_____
_____

### Emotions Before Sleep

_____

### Dream

_____
_____
_____
_____
_____
_____
_____

### Interpretation

_____
_____

### Feeling Upon Awakening

_____
_____
_____

### Comments

_____
_____
_____

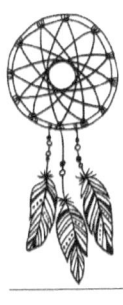

# Dream Journal

Date:_____     Time:_____

## Thoughts Before Sleep

_____
_____
_____
_____
_____

## Emotions Before Sleep

_____

## Dream

_____
_____
_____
_____
_____
_____
_____
_____

## Interpretation

_____
_____
_____

## Feeling Upon Awakening

_____
_____
_____

## Comments

_____
_____
_____

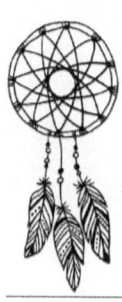

# Dream Journal

Date:_____          Time:_____

### Thoughts Before Sleep

_____
_____
_____
_____
_____

### Emotions Before Sleep

_____

### Dream

_____
_____
_____
_____
_____
_____
_____

### Interpretation

_____
_____
_____

### Feeling Upon Awakening

_____
_____
_____

### Comments

_____
_____
_____

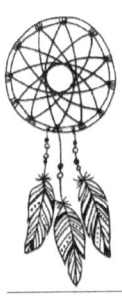

# Dream Journal

Date:_____          Time:_____

## Thoughts Before Sleep

_____
_____
_____
_____
_____

## Emotions Before Sleep

_____

## Dream

_____
_____
_____
_____
_____
_____
_____
_____

## Interpretation

_____
_____

## Feeling Upon Awakening

_____
_____
_____

## Comments

_____
_____
_____

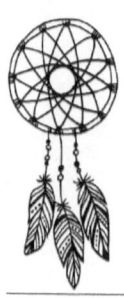

# Dream Journal

Date:_____          Time:_____

## Thoughts Before Sleep

_____
_____
_____
_____
_____

## Emotions Before Sleep

_____

## Dream

_____
_____
_____
_____
_____
_____
_____

## Interpretation

_____
_____
_____

## Feeling Upon Awakening

_____
_____
_____
_____

## Comments

_____
_____
_____

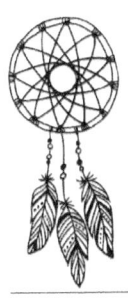

# Dream Journal

Date:_____          Time:_____

## Thoughts Before Sleep

_____
_____
_____
_____
_____

## Emotions Before Sleep

_____

## Dream

_____
_____
_____
_____
_____
_____
_____

## Interpretation

_____
_____

## Feeling Upon Awakening

_____
_____
_____

## Comments

_____
_____
_____

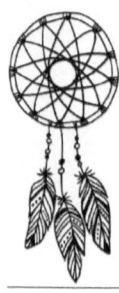

# Dream Journal

Date:_____          Time:_____

### Thoughts Before Sleep

_____
_____
_____
_____
_____

### Emotions Before Sleep

_____

### Dream

_____
_____
_____
_____
_____
_____
_____

### Interpretation

_____
_____
_____

### Feeling Upon Awakening

_____
_____
_____
_____

### Comments

_____
_____
_____

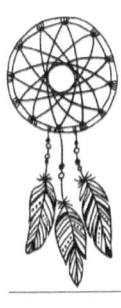

# Dream Journal

Date:_____          Time:_____

## Thoughts Before Sleep

_____

_____

_____

_____

_____

## Emotions Before Sleep

_____

## Dream

_____

_____

_____

_____

_____

_____

_____

_____

## Interpretation

_____

_____

_____

## Feeling Upon Awakening

_____

_____

_____

## Comments

_____

_____

_____

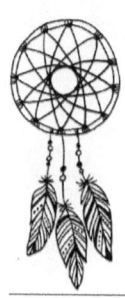

# Dream Journal

Date:_____          Time:_____

### Thoughts Before Sleep

_____
_____
_____
_____
_____

### Emotions Before Sleep

_____

### Dream

_____
_____
_____
_____
_____
_____

### Interpretation

_____
_____
_____

### Feeling Upon Awakening

_____
_____
_____

### Comments

_____
_____
_____

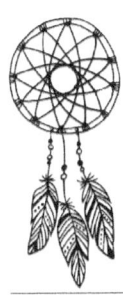

# Dream Journal

Date:_____          Time:_____

## Thoughts Before Sleep

_____
_____
_____
_____
_____

## Emotions Before Sleep

_____

## Dream

_____
_____
_____
_____
_____
_____
_____
_____
_____

## Interpretation

_____
_____
_____

## Feeling Upon Awakening

_____
_____
_____

## Comments

_____
_____
_____
_____

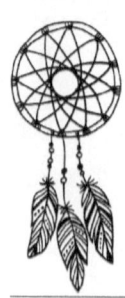

# Dream Journal

Date:_____          Time:_____

## Thoughts Before Sleep

_____
_____
_____
_____
_____

## Emotions Before Sleep

_____

## Dream

_____
_____
_____
_____
_____
_____
_____

## Interpretation

_____
_____
_____

## Feeling Upon Awakening

_____
_____
_____
_____

## Comments

_____
_____
_____

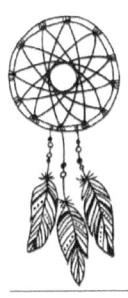

# Dream Journal

Date:_____          Time:_____

## Thoughts Before Sleep

_____
_____
_____
_____
_____

## Emotions Before Sleep

_____

## Dream

_____
_____
_____
_____
_____
_____
_____

## Interpretation

_____
_____

## Feeling Upon Awakening

_____
_____
_____

## Comments

_____
_____
_____

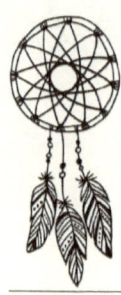

# Dream Journal

Date:_____                    Time:_____

### Thoughts Before Sleep

_____
_____
_____
_____

### Emotions Before Sleep

_____

### Dream

_____
_____
_____
_____
_____
_____
_____

### Interpretation

_____
_____

### Feeling Upon Awakening

_____
_____

### Comments

_____
_____
_____

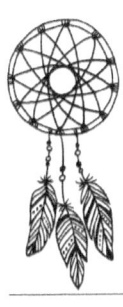

# Dream Journal

Date:_____          Time:_____

## Thoughts Before Sleep

_____
_____
_____
_____

## Emotions Before Sleep

_____

## Dream

_____
_____
_____
_____
_____
_____
_____

## Interpretation

_____
_____
_____

## Feeling Upon Awakening

_____
_____
_____

## Comments

_____
_____
_____

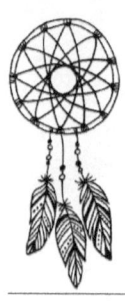

# Dream Journal

Date:_____          Time:_____

## Thoughts Before Sleep

_____
_____
_____
_____
_____

## Emotions Before Sleep

_____

## Dream

_____
_____
_____
_____
_____
_____
_____

## Interpretation

_____
_____
_____

## Feeling Upon Awakening

_____
_____
_____

## Comments

_____
_____
_____

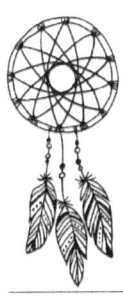

# Dream Journal

Date:_____        Time:_____

### Thoughts Before Sleep

_____
_____
_____
_____
_____

### Emotions Before Sleep

_____

### Dream

_____
_____
_____
_____
_____
_____
_____

### Interpretation

_____
_____

### Feeling Upon Awakening

_____
_____
_____

### Comments

_____
_____
_____

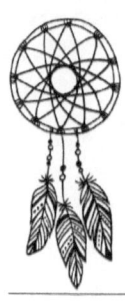

# Dream Journal

Date:_____          Time:_____

## Thoughts Before Sleep

_____
_____
_____
_____
_____

## Emotions Before Sleep

_____

## Dream

_____
_____
_____
_____
_____
_____

## Interpretation

_____
_____
_____

## Feeling Upon Awakening

_____
_____
_____

## Comments

_____
_____
_____

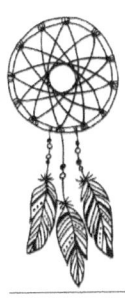

# Dream Journal

Date:_____          Time:_____

## Thoughts Before Sleep

_____
_____
_____
_____
_____

## Emotions Before Sleep

_____

## Dream

_____
_____
_____
_____
_____
_____
_____
_____

## Interpretation

_____
_____
_____

## Feeling Upon Awakening

_____
_____
_____

## Comments

_____
_____
_____

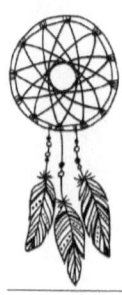

# Dream Journal

Date:_____                    Time:_____

## Thoughts Before Sleep

_____
_____
_____
_____
_____

## Emotions Before Sleep

_____

## Dream

_____
_____
_____
_____
_____
_____
_____

## Interpretation

_____
_____
_____

## Feeling Upon Awakening

_____
_____
_____
_____

## Comments

_____
_____
_____

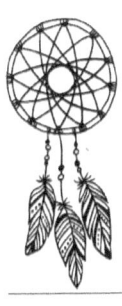

# Dream Journal

Date:_____     Time:_____

## Thoughts Before Sleep

_____
_____
_____
_____
_____

## Emotions Before Sleep

_____

## Dream

_____
_____
_____
_____
_____
_____
_____

## Interpretation

_____
_____

## Feeling Upon Awakening

_____
_____
_____

## Comments

_____
_____
_____

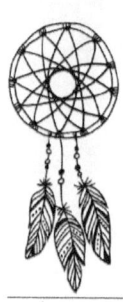

# Dream Journal

Date:_____          Time:_____

## Thoughts Before Sleep

_____
_____
_____
_____
_____

## Emotions Before Sleep

_____

## Dream

_____
_____
_____
_____
_____
_____

## Interpretation

_____
_____
_____

## Feeling Upon Awakening

_____
_____
_____

## Comments

_____
_____
_____

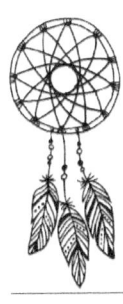

# Dream Journal

Date:_____          Time:_____

## Thoughts Before Sleep

_____
_____
_____
_____
_____

## Emotions Before Sleep

_____

## Dream

_____
_____
_____
_____
_____
_____
_____
_____

## Interpretation

_____
_____

## Feeling Upon Awakening

_____
_____
_____

## Comments

_____
_____
_____

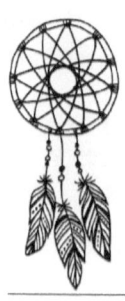

# Dream Journal

Date:_____     Time:_____

## Thoughts Before Sleep

_____
_____
_____
_____
_____

## Emotions Before Sleep

_____

## Dream

_____
_____
_____
_____
_____
_____
_____

## Interpretation

_____
_____
_____

## Feeling Upon Awakening

_____
_____
_____

## Comments

_____
_____
_____

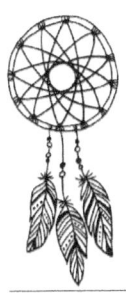

# Dream Journal

Date:_____          Time:_____

### Thoughts Before Sleep

_____
_____
_____
_____
_____

### Emotions Before Sleep

_____

### Dream

_____
_____
_____
_____
_____
_____
_____
_____

### Interpretation

_____
_____

### Feeling Upon Awakening

_____
_____
_____

### Comments

_____
_____
_____

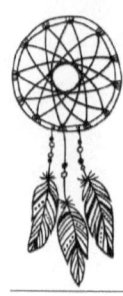

# Dream Journal

Date:_____ Time:_____

### Thoughts Before Sleep

_____
_____
_____
_____
_____

### Emotions Before Sleep

_____

### Dream

_____
_____
_____
_____
_____
_____
_____

### Interpretation

_____
_____

### Feeling Upon Awakening

_____
_____
_____

### Comments

_____
_____
_____

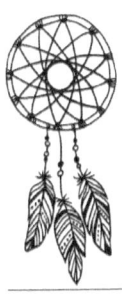

# Dream Journal

Date:_____        Time:_____

## Thoughts Before Sleep

_____
_____
_____
_____
_____

## Emotions Before Sleep

_____

## Dream

_____
_____
_____
_____
_____
_____
_____

## Interpretation

_____
_____

## Feeling Upon Awakening

_____
_____
_____

## Comments

_____
_____
_____

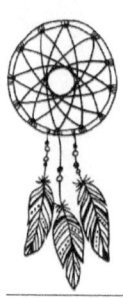

# Dream Journal

Date:_____ Time:_____

## Thoughts Before Sleep

_____
_____
_____
_____
_____

## Emotions Before Sleep

_____

## Dream

_____
_____
_____
_____
_____
_____
_____

## Interpretation

_____
_____
_____

## Feeling Upon Awakening

_____
_____
_____

## Comments

_____
_____
_____

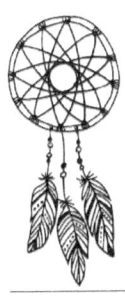

# Dream Journal

Date:_____          Time:_____

### Thoughts Before Sleep

_____
_____
_____
_____
_____

### Emotions Before Sleep

_____

### Dream

_____
_____
_____
_____
_____
_____
_____

### Interpretation

_____
_____
_____

### Feeling Upon Awakening

_____
_____
_____

### Comments

_____
_____
_____

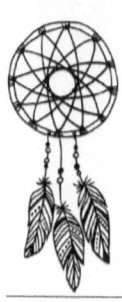

# Dream Journal

Date:_____                    Time:_____

### Thoughts Before Sleep

_____
_____
_____
_____
_____

### Emotions Before Sleep

_____

### Dream

_____
_____
_____
_____
_____
_____
_____

### Interpretation

_____
_____
_____

### Feeling Upon Awakening

_____
_____
_____

### Comments

_____
_____
_____

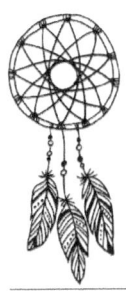

# Dream Journal

Date:_____          Time:_____

## Thoughts Before Sleep

_____
_____
_____
_____
_____

## Emotions Before Sleep

_____

## Dream

_____
_____
_____
_____
_____
_____
_____
_____

## Interpretation

_____
_____

## Feeling Upon Awakening

_____
_____
_____

## Comments

_____
_____
_____

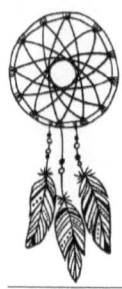

# Dream Journal

Date:_____          Time:_____

## Thoughts Before Sleep

_____
_____
_____
_____
_____

## Emotions Before Sleep

_____

## Dream

_____
_____
_____
_____
_____
_____
_____

## Interpretation

_____
_____

## Feeling Upon Awakening

_____
_____
_____

## Comments

_____
_____

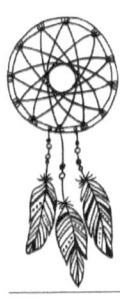

# Dream Journal

Date:_____          Time:_____

## Thoughts Before Sleep

_____
_____
_____
_____
_____

## Emotions Before Sleep

_____

## Dream

_____
_____
_____
_____
_____
_____
_____

## Interpretation

_____
_____
_____

## Feeling Upon Awakening

_____
_____
_____

## Comments

_____
_____
_____

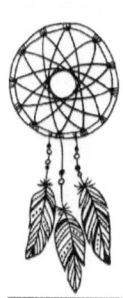

# Dream Journal

Date:_____          Time:_____

## Thoughts Before Sleep

_____
_____
_____
_____
_____

## Emotions Before Sleep

_____

## Dream

_____
_____
_____
_____
_____
_____
_____

## Interpretation

_____
_____

## Feeling Upon Awakening

_____
_____
_____

## Comments

_____
_____
_____

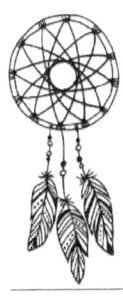

# Dream Journal

Date:_____          Time:_____

## Thoughts Before Sleep

_____
_____
_____
_____
_____

## Emotions Before Sleep

_____

## Dream

_____
_____
_____
_____
_____
_____
_____

## Interpretation

_____
_____

## Feeling Upon Awakening

_____
_____
_____

## Comments

_____
_____
_____

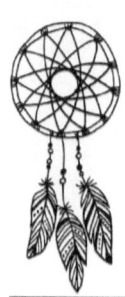

# Dream Journal

Date:_____          Time:_____

## Thoughts Before Sleep

_____
_____
_____
_____
_____

## Emotions Before Sleep

_____

## Dream

_____
_____
_____
_____
_____
_____
_____

## Interpretation

_____
_____
_____

## Feeling Upon Awakening

_____
_____
_____

## Comments

_____
_____
_____

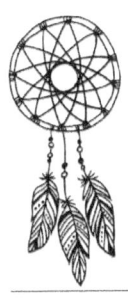

# Dream Journal

Date:_____          Time:_____

## Thoughts Before Sleep

_____
_____
_____
_____
_____

## Emotions Before Sleep

_____

## Dream

_____
_____
_____
_____
_____
_____
_____
_____

## Interpretation

_____
_____

## Feeling Upon Awakening

_____
_____
_____

## Comments

_____
_____
_____

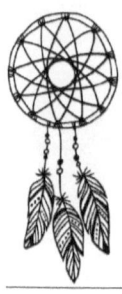

# Dream Journal

Date:_____          Time:_____

## Thoughts Before Sleep

_____
_____
_____
_____
_____

## Emotions Before Sleep

_____

## Dream

_____
_____
_____
_____
_____
_____
_____

## Interpretation

_____
_____

## Feeling Upon Awakening

_____
_____
_____

## Comments

_____
_____
_____

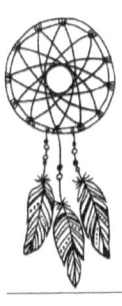

# Dream Journal

Date:_____          Time:_____

## Thoughts Before Sleep

_____
_____
_____
_____
_____

## Emotions Before Sleep

_____

## Dream

_____
_____
_____
_____
_____
_____
_____

## Interpretation

_____
_____
_____

## Feeling Upon Awakening

_____
_____
_____

## Comments

_____
_____
_____

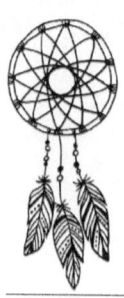

# Dream Journal

Date:_____          Time:_____

## Thoughts Before Sleep

_____
_____
_____
_____
_____

## Emotions Before Sleep

_____

## Dream

_____
_____
_____
_____
_____
_____

## Interpretation

_____
_____

## Feeling Upon Awakening

_____
_____
_____

## Comments

_____
_____
_____

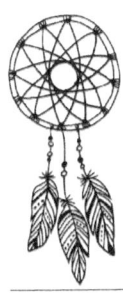

# Dream Journal

Date:_____          Time:_____

## Thoughts Before Sleep

_____
_____
_____
_____
_____

## Emotions Before Sleep

_____

## Dream

_____
_____
_____
_____
_____
_____
_____

## Interpretation

_____
_____

## Feeling Upon Awakening

_____
_____
_____

## Comments

_____
_____
_____

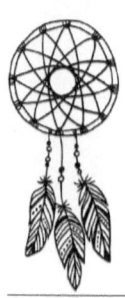

# Dream Journal

Date:_____                          Time:_____

## Thoughts Before Sleep

_____
_____
_____
_____
_____

## Emotions Before Sleep

_____

## Dream

_____
_____
_____
_____
_____
_____
_____

## Interpretation

_____
_____
_____

## Feeling Upon Awakening

_____
_____
_____

## Comments

_____
_____
_____

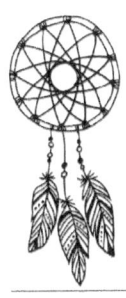

# Dream Journal

Date:_____          Time:_____

## Thoughts Before Sleep

_____
_____
_____
_____
_____

## Emotions Before Sleep

_____

## Dream

_____
_____
_____
_____
_____
_____
_____
_____

## Interpretation

_____
_____
_____

## Feeling Upon Awakening

_____
_____
_____

## Comments

_____
_____
_____

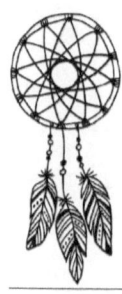

# Dream Journal

Date:_____          Time:_____

### Thoughts Before Sleep

_____
_____
_____
_____
_____

### Emotions Before Sleep

_____

### Dream

_____
_____
_____
_____
_____
_____
_____

### Interpretation

_____
_____
_____

### Feeling Upon Awakening

_____
_____
_____

### Comments

_____
_____
_____

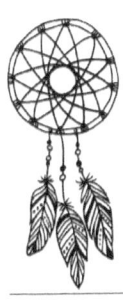

# Dream Journal

Date:_____          Time:_____

## Thoughts Before Sleep

_____
_____
_____
_____
_____

## Emotions Before Sleep

_____

## Dream

_____
_____
_____
_____
_____
_____
_____

## Interpretation

_____
_____
_____

## Feeling Upon Awakening

_____
_____
_____

## Comments

_____
_____
_____

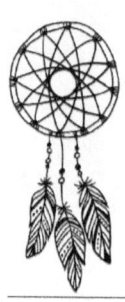

# Dream Journal

Date:_____ Time:_____

## Thoughts Before Sleep

_____
_____
_____
_____
_____

## Emotions Before Sleep

_____

## Dream

_____
_____
_____
_____
_____
_____
_____

## Interpretation

_____
_____
_____

## Feeling Upon Awakening

_____
_____
_____

## Comments

_____
_____
_____

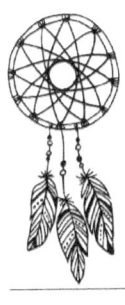

# Dream Journal

Date:_____          Time:_____

## Thoughts Before Sleep

_____
_____
_____
_____
_____

## Emotions Before Sleep

_____

## Dream

_____
_____
_____
_____
_____
_____
_____

## Interpretation

_____
_____

## Feeling Upon Awakening

_____
_____
_____

## Comments

_____
_____
_____

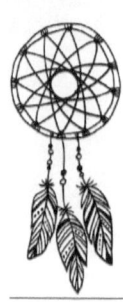

# Dream Journal

Date:_____     Time:_____

## Thoughts Before Sleep

_____
_____
_____
_____
_____

## Emotions Before Sleep

_____

## Dream

_____
_____
_____
_____
_____
_____
_____

## Interpretation

_____
_____
_____

## Feeling Upon Awakening

_____
_____
_____

## Comments

_____
_____
_____

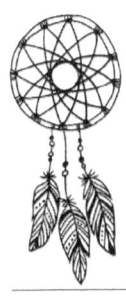

# Dream Journal

Date:_____          Time:_____

## Thoughts Before Sleep

_____
_____
_____
_____
_____

## Emotions Before Sleep

_____

## Dream

_____
_____
_____
_____
_____
_____
_____
_____

## Interpretation

_____
_____
_____

## Feeling Upon Awakening

_____
_____
_____

## Comments

_____
_____
_____

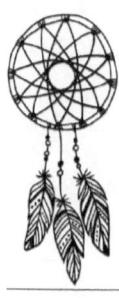

# Dream Journal

Date:_____     Time:_____

## Thoughts Before Sleep

_____
_____
_____
_____
_____

## Emotions Before Sleep

_____

## Dream

_____
_____
_____
_____
_____
_____
_____

## Interpretation

_____
_____
_____

## Feeling Upon Awakening

_____
_____
_____
_____

## Comments

_____
_____
_____

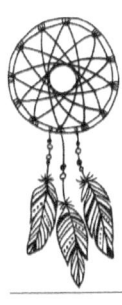

# Dream Journal

Date:_____          Time:_____

## Thoughts Before Sleep

_____
_____
_____
_____
_____

## Emotions Before Sleep

_____
_____

## Dream

_____
_____
_____
_____
_____
_____
_____
_____

## Interpretation

_____
_____
_____

## Feeling Upon Awakening

_____
_____
_____

## Comments

_____
_____
_____

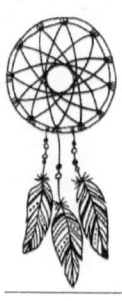

# Dream Journal

Date:_____                    Time:_____

## Thoughts Before Sleep

_____
_____
_____
_____
_____

## Emotions Before Sleep

_____

## Dream

_____
_____
_____
_____
_____
_____

## Interpretation

_____
_____
_____

## Feeling Upon Awakening

_____
_____
_____

## Comments

_____
_____
_____

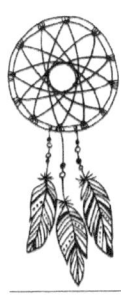

# Dream Journal

Date:_____          Time:_____

## Thoughts Before Sleep

_____
_____
_____
_____
_____

## Emotions Before Sleep

_____

## Dream

_____
_____
_____
_____
_____
_____
_____

## Interpretation

_____
_____
_____

## Feeling Upon Awakening

_____
_____
_____

## Comments

_____
_____
_____

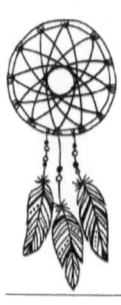

# Dream Journal

Date:_____          Time:_____

## Thoughts Before Sleep

_____
_____
_____
_____
_____

## Emotions Before Sleep

_____

## Dream

_____
_____
_____
_____
_____
_____

## Interpretation

_____
_____
_____

## Feeling Upon Awakening

_____
_____
_____

## Comments

_____
_____
_____

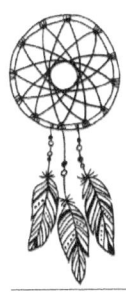

# Dream Journal

Date:_____ Time:_____

## Thoughts Before Sleep

_____
_____
_____
_____
_____

## Emotions Before Sleep

_____

## Dream

_____
_____
_____
_____
_____
_____
_____
_____

## Interpretation

_____
_____

## Feeling Upon Awakening

_____
_____
_____

## Comments

_____
_____
_____

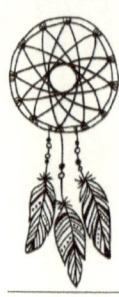

# Dream Journal

Date:_____          Time:_____

### Thoughts Before Sleep

_____
_____
_____
_____
_____

### Emotions Before Sleep

_____

### Dream

_____
_____
_____
_____
_____
_____
_____
_____

### Interpretation

_____
_____
_____

### Feeling Upon Awakening

_____
_____
_____

### Comments

_____
_____
_____

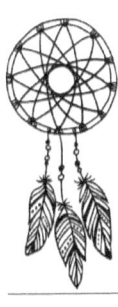

# Dream Journal

Date:_____          Time:_____

## Thoughts Before Sleep

_____

_____

_____

_____

## Emotions Before Sleep

_____

## Dream

_____

_____

_____

_____

_____

_____

_____

## Interpretation

_____

_____

## Feeling Upon Awakening

_____

_____

_____

## Comments

_____

_____

_____

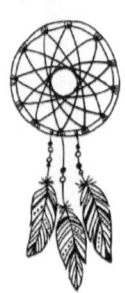

# Dream Journal

Date:_____                          Time:_____

## Thoughts Before Sleep

_____
_____
_____
_____
_____

## Emotions Before Sleep

_____

## Dream

_____
_____
_____
_____
_____
_____
_____

## Interpretation

_____
_____

## Feeling Upon Awakening

_____
_____
_____

## Comments

_____
_____
_____

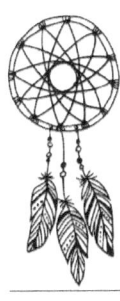

# Dream Journal

Date:_____          Time:_____

## Thoughts Before Sleep

_____
_____
_____
_____
_____

## Emotions Before Sleep

_____

## Dream

_____
_____
_____
_____
_____
_____
_____
_____

## Interpretation

_____
_____
_____

## Feeling Upon Awakening

_____
_____
_____

## Comments

_____
_____
_____

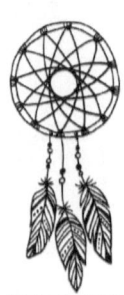

# Dream Journal

Date:_____          Time:_____

### Thoughts Before Sleep

_____
_____
_____
_____
_____

### Emotions Before Sleep

_____

### Dream

_____
_____
_____
_____
_____
_____
_____

### Interpretation

_____
_____
_____

### Feeling Upon Awakening

_____
_____
_____

### Comments

_____
_____
_____

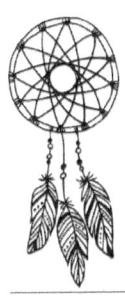

# Dream Journal

Date:_____          Time:_____

## Thoughts Before Sleep

_____
_____
_____
_____
_____

## Emotions Before Sleep

_____

## Dream

_____
_____
_____
_____
_____
_____
_____
_____

## Interpretation

_____
_____
_____

## Feeling Upon Awakening

_____
_____
_____

## Comments

_____
_____
_____

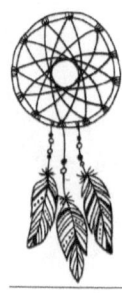

# Dream Journal

Date:_____          Time:_____

## Thoughts Before Sleep

_____
_____
_____
_____
_____

## Emotions Before Sleep

_____

## Dream

_____
_____
_____
_____
_____
_____
_____

## Interpretation

_____
_____

## Feeling Upon Awakening

_____
_____
_____

## Comments

_____
_____
_____

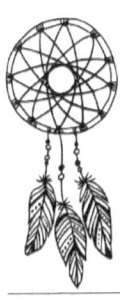

# Dream Journal

Date:_____          Time:_____

## Thoughts Before Sleep

_____
_____
_____
_____
_____

## Emotions Before Sleep

_____

## Dream

_____
_____
_____
_____
_____
_____
_____

## Interpretation

_____
_____
_____

## Feeling Upon Awakening

_____
_____
_____

## Comments

_____
_____
_____

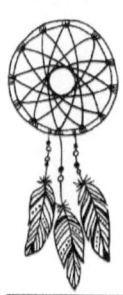

# Dream Journal

Date:_____            Time:_____

## Thoughts Before Sleep

_____
_____
_____
_____
_____

## Emotions Before Sleep

_____

## Dream

_____
_____
_____
_____
_____
_____
_____

## Interpretation

_____
_____
_____

## Feeling Upon Awakening

_____
_____
_____

## Comments

_____
_____
_____

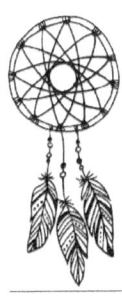

# Dream Journal

Date:_____          Time:_____

## Thoughts Before Sleep

_____
_____
_____
_____
_____

## Emotions Before Sleep

_____

## Dream

_____
_____
_____
_____
_____
_____
_____

## Interpretation

_____
_____

## Feeling Upon Awakening

_____
_____
_____

## Comments

_____
_____
_____

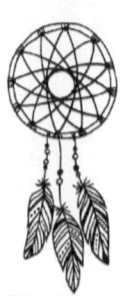

# Dream Journal

Date:_____          Time:_____

## Thoughts Before Sleep

_____

_____

_____

_____

_____

## Emotions Before Sleep

_____

## Dream

_____

_____

_____

_____

_____

_____

_____

## Interpretation

_____

_____

_____

## Feeling Upon Awakening

_____

_____

_____

## Comments

_____

_____

_____

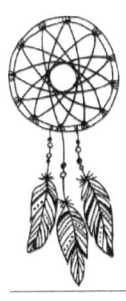

# Dream Journal

Date:_____ Time:_____

## Thoughts Before Sleep

_____
_____
_____
_____
_____

## Emotions Before Sleep

_____

## Dream

_____
_____
_____
_____
_____
_____
_____

## Interpretation

_____
_____

## Feeling Upon Awakening

_____
_____
_____

## Comments

_____
_____
_____

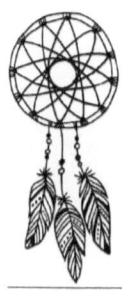

# Dream Journal

Date:_____                          Time:_____

## Thoughts Before Sleep

_____
_____
_____
_____
_____

## Emotions Before Sleep

_____

## Dream

_____
_____
_____
_____
_____
_____
_____

## Interpretation

_____
_____

## Feeling Upon Awakening

_____
_____
_____

## Comments

_____
_____
_____

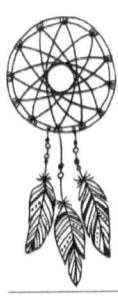

# Dream Journal

Date:_____          Time:_____

## Thoughts Before Sleep

_____
_____
_____
_____
_____

## Emotions Before Sleep

_____

## Dream

_____
_____
_____
_____
_____
_____
_____

## Interpretation

_____
_____
_____

## Feeling Upon Awakening

_____
_____
_____

## Comments

_____
_____
_____

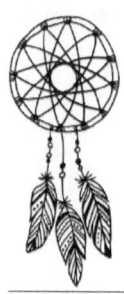

# Dream Journal

Date:_____                    Time:_____

## Thoughts Before Sleep

_____
_____
_____
_____
_____

## Emotions Before Sleep

_____

## Dream

_____
_____
_____
_____
_____
_____
_____

## Interpretation

_____
_____

## Feeling Upon Awakening

_____
_____
_____

## Comments

_____
_____

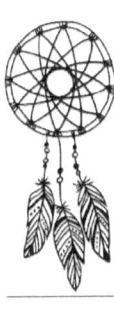

# Dream Journal

Date:_____       Time:_____

## Thoughts Before Sleep

_____
_____
_____
_____
_____

## Emotions Before Sleep

_____

## Dream

_____
_____
_____
_____
_____
_____
_____

## Interpretation

_____
_____

## Feeling Upon Awakening

_____
_____
_____

## Comments

_____
_____
_____

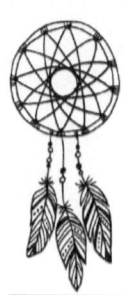

# Dream Journal

Date:_____ Time:_____

## Thoughts Before Sleep

_____
_____
_____
_____
_____

## Emotions Before Sleep

_____

## Dream

_____
_____
_____
_____
_____
_____
_____

## Interpretation

_____
_____
_____

## Feeling Upon Awakening

_____
_____
_____

## Comments

_____
_____
_____

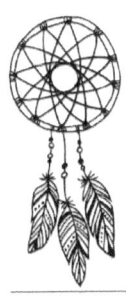

# Dream Journal

Date:_____ Time:_____

## Thoughts Before Sleep

_____
_____
_____
_____
_____

## Emotions Before Sleep

_____

## Dream

_____
_____
_____
_____
_____
_____
_____

## Interpretation

_____
_____
_____

## Feeling Upon Awakening

_____
_____
_____

## Comments

_____
_____
_____

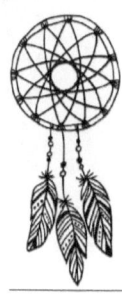

# Dream Journal

Date:_____                    Time:_____

## Thoughts Before Sleep

_____
_____
_____
_____
_____

## Emotions Before Sleep

_____

## Dream

_____
_____
_____
_____
_____
_____
_____

## Interpretation

_____
_____
_____

## Feeling Upon Awakening

_____
_____
_____

## Comments

_____
_____
_____

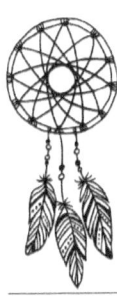

# Dream Journal

Date:_____          Time:_____

## Thoughts Before Sleep

_____
_____
_____
_____
_____

## Emotions Before Sleep

_____

## Dream

_____
_____
_____
_____
_____
_____
_____

## Interpretation

_____
_____
_____

## Feeling Upon Awakening

_____
_____
_____

## Comments

_____
_____
_____

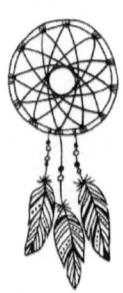

# Dream Journal

Date:_____ Time:_____

## Thoughts Before Sleep

_____
_____
_____
_____
_____

## Emotions Before Sleep

_____

## Dream

_____
_____
_____
_____
_____
_____
_____

## Interpretation

_____
_____
_____

## Feeling Upon Awakening

_____
_____
_____

## Comments

_____
_____
_____

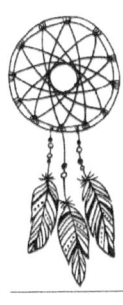

# Dream Journal

Date:_____          Time:_____

### Thoughts Before Sleep

_____
_____
_____
_____
_____

### Emotions Before Sleep

_____

### Dream

_____
_____
_____
_____
_____
_____
_____
_____

### Interpretation

_____
_____

### Feeling Upon Awakening

_____
_____
_____

### Comments

_____
_____
_____

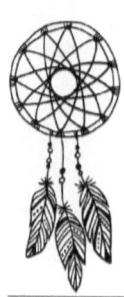

# Dream Journal

Date:_____                    Time:_____

## Thoughts Before Sleep

_____
_____
_____
_____
_____

## Emotions Before Sleep

_____

## Dream

_____
_____
_____
_____
_____
_____
_____

## Interpretation

_____
_____

## Feeling Upon Awakening

_____
_____
_____

## Comments

_____
_____
_____

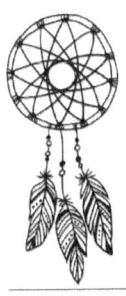

# Dream Journal

Date:_____                    Time:_____

### Thoughts Before Sleep

_____
_____
_____
_____
_____

### Emotions Before Sleep

_____

### Dream

_____
_____
_____
_____
_____
_____
_____
_____

### Interpretation

_____
_____

### Feeling Upon Awakening

_____
_____
_____

### Comments

_____
_____
_____

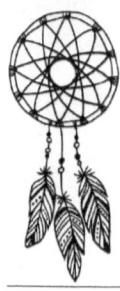

# Dream Journal

Date:_____　　　　　　　Time:_____

### Thoughts Before Sleep

_____
_____
_____
_____

### Emotions Before Sleep

_____

### Dream

_____
_____
_____
_____
_____
_____
_____

### Interpretation

_____
_____

### Feeling Upon Awakening

_____
_____
_____

### Comments

_____
_____
_____

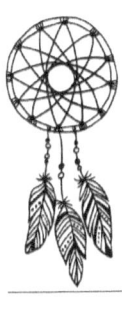

# Dream Journal

Date:_____          Time:_____

## Thoughts Before Sleep

_____
_____
_____
_____

## Emotions Before Sleep

_____

## Dream

_____
_____
_____
_____
_____
_____

## Interpretation

_____
_____

## Feeling Upon Awakening

_____
_____
_____

## Comments

_____
_____
_____

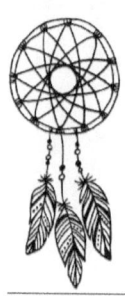

# Dream Journal

Date:_____          Time:_____

## Thoughts Before Sleep

_____
_____
_____
_____
_____

## Emotions Before Sleep

_____

## Dream

_____
_____
_____
_____
_____
_____
_____

## Interpretation

_____
_____

## Feeling Upon Awakening

_____
_____
_____

## Comments

_____
_____
_____

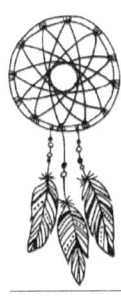

# Dream Journal

Date:_____          Time:_____

## Thoughts Before Sleep

_____
_____
_____
_____
_____

## Emotions Before Sleep

_____

## Dream

_____
_____
_____
_____
_____
_____
_____

## Interpretation

_____
_____

## Feeling Upon Awakening

_____
_____
_____

## Comments

_____
_____
_____

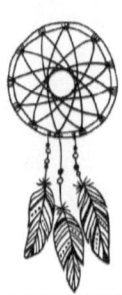

# Dream Journal

Date:_____          Time:_____

## Thoughts Before Sleep

_____
_____
_____
_____
_____

## Emotions Before Sleep

_____

## Dream

_____
_____
_____
_____
_____
_____

## Interpretation

_____
_____

## Feeling Upon Awakening

_____
_____
_____

## Comments

_____
_____
_____

www.ingramcontent.com/pod-product-compliance
Lightning Source LLC
Chambersburg PA
CBHW020555220526
45463CB00006B/2318